A Colony of Seals

THE CAPTIVATING LIFE OF A DEEP SEA DIVER

BY VICKI LEÓN

LONDON TOWN PRESS

The London Town *Wild Life* Series
Series Editor
Vicki León

A Colony of Seals
Principal photographer
Frank Balthis

Additional photographers
Ralph A. Clevenger; Howard Hall; Richard R. Hansen;
W. E. Townsend, Jr.

London Town Press
P.O. Box 585
Montrose, California 91021
www.LondonTownPress.com

Book design by Christy Hale
10   9   8   7   6   5   4   3   2   1

Printed in Singapore

Distributed by Publishers Group West

Publisher's Cataloging-in-Publication Data
León, Vicki.
A colony of seals : the captivating life of a deep sea diver /
Vicki León ; photographs by Frank Balthis [et al.] —2nd ed.
p.   cm. — (London Town wild life series)
Originally published: San Luis Obispo, CA : Blake Books
©1993.
Summary: Describes the life cycles, behaviors and habitats
of harbor seals, California sea lions, and elephant seals, with
full-color photographs.
Includes bibliographic references and index.
ISBN 0-9766134-0-9
1. Harbor seal—Juvenile literature.   2. California sea lion—
Juvenile literature.   3. Northern elephant seal—Juvenile
literature.   4. Southern elephant seal—Juvenile literature.
[1. Harbor seal. 2. California sea lion. 3. Elephant seal.]
I. Balthis, Frank. II. Title. Series.
QL737.P6 L46 2005
599.79—dc22
2005930183

FRONT COVER: Once a year, a northern elephant seal molts,
shedding skin and fur. Flexible flippers let this young seal
scratch where it itches.

TITLE PAGE: A young elephant seal displays its flexible spine.
This adaptation allows it to chase speedy squid underwater—
and to move its heavy body on land.

BACK COVER: When foraging, a California sea lion hunts for
days at a time. While at sea, its muscular body and breath-
holding abilities let it dive often without taking a rest.

Contents

Flippered "bears of the sea"

The chubby marine mammals we know as seals are more accurately called pinnipeds, or "fin-footed ones." Scientists divide them into three families: true seals, eared seals, and walruses. This book offers a closeup look at four familiar members of these relatives: the harbor seal (a true seal), the California sea lion (an eared seal), and the northern and southern elephant seals (both eared seals).

All pinnipeds come from an ancient ancestor called Enaliarctos, meaning "bear of the sea." The size of a harbor seal, it had bearlike teeth and used flippers to swim. Pinnipeds have also earned the nickname of another land animal: Spanish settlers in California called them *lobos marinos*,

◄ Elephant seal juveniles enjoy each others' company. Some pups are nicknamed "super weaners," because they steal milk and get hugely fat, swelling to 400 pounds in six weeks.

or "sea wolves." Neither bears nor wolves, today's pinnipeds have evolved into 33 species, now occupying nearly all of the earth's oceans–and a few lakes as well.

Although marine mammals, most seal species also have an eventful life on land. Seals go ashore in large groups for two to six months, some migrating great distances to reach these breeding grounds. There they mate, give birth, nurse pups, and molt.

Afterward, most seals return to the open ocean. Their wanderings may take them to the icy shores of the Arctic or around the Antarctic. Each animal swims vast distances, following its food supply, hunting on its own.

While tracking prey, many pinnipeds routinely dive deeper than most whales— and for longer periods, too. Elephant seals are the champs. They descend thousands of feet, their bodies able to withstand the crushing pressure one mile under the sea.

Although seals breathe air as we do, many can stay underwater for 30 minutes or more. Elephant seals again hold the record, remaining below as long as 120 minutes. The adaptations these animals have made to extremes of temperature and

▶ Near the ocean floor, a California sea lion swims, using its strong foreflippers to speed it along. Hindflippers help steer the animal.

pressure amaze scientists, who hope to discover their secrets.

Pinniped species have distinct looks and behaviors. The leopard seal is a slim, sinister eating machine. The hooded seal male sports an inflatable red nose like a clown's. Fur seals are nicknamed "sea bears" for their two layers of fur, while elephant seals have little hair. The bearded seal is a solitary creature, giving birth on Arctic pack ice and weaning its pup in 18 days. Walruses, on the other hand, are social, migrating in herds, and protecting and nursing their young for two years.

In general, pinnipeds share a common body shape—well-padded, streamlined, and round as a barrel. They flash through the water with grace and speed.

Members of the true seal family have short, paddle-shaped front limbs, but cover a surprising amount of ground. On sand, some wiggle on their bellies, going

◀ When at a rookery or breeding ground like Ano Nuevo, California, adult elephant seals do not eat or drink for three months. To save energy for mating, fighting, and nursing pups, the animals rest often.

100 feet a minute. The ribbon seal skims across the ice faster than a person can run. Eared seals on land, including fur seals and sea lions, move in a more upright fashion, bounding along at 12 miles per hour. Walruses use their long tusks to haul themselves onto ice floes. Some two-ton pinnipeds can even climb steep sand dunes or cliffs.

Pinnipeds share another, sadder bond. Like the great whales, many seal species were hunted to near extinction in the 19th and 20th centuries for their fur and blubber. Now protected by international laws, most have recovered. Some have been lost. And some populations remain endangered, from Steller's sea lions to several of the monk seals, and need human help to survive.

▲ Under the sea, the eyes of a sea lion glow purple. All pinnipeds have a mirrorlike crystal, or tapetum, in both eyes. This lets them see well underwater and at night.

The remarkable variety in pinnipeds' appearance starts at the top. Many kinds of seals have round heads with no necks. Many others have doglike heads, with longer muzzles. You can spot male sea lions by the bony growth on the head, called a sagittal crest.

Seal eyes are large—up to three inches in diameter. That gives them excellent vision, in air and underwater. Pinniped ears, whether internal (like those of the walrus and harbor seal) or external (like those of sea lions and fur seals) have special modifications, letting them pinpoint sounds in the ocean.

Nostrils can lock shut, an advantage when diving. A female seal relies on smell as well as vocal signals to recognize her pups. Near its mouth and above its eyes, a seal has whiskers as sensitive as fingers, useful for locating prey in murky water or darkness.

Seals are opportunistic carnivores, with sharp teeth able to take advantage of what's available. Monk seals roam warm waters, hunting lobster and octopus. Leopard seals are loners that pounce on penguins, fish, and other seals. Fur seals eat cod, herring, and seabirds on occasion. The walrus gets fat on a diet of clams and other ocean floor creatures, which it sucks up in vacuum-cleaner fashion.

The skin of most pinnipeds is covered with fur. Underneath, pinnipeds wear a layer of blubber, three to four inches thick. Blubber is dandy stuff. It keeps the animal warm, streamlines its shape, and keeps the body from being crushed during deep dives.

▼ The nose on a harbor seal can close tightly, a big help when diving. Its long whiskers help it find octopus and other prey.

◄ A meat-eater, an elephant seal uses whiskers to locate prey and 32 teeth to grab it. Its canines can be eight inches long. Prey, from dogfish shark to squid, is swallowed in one gulp.

Blubber is also a critical food supply. Most species do not eat while breeding or molting. Instead, they live on their own fat for months. Female pinnipeds also draw from their blubber to produce lots of fat-rich milk for their young.

Foreflippers and hindflippers are vital for underwater agility. Pinnipeds move their bodies side to side, with foreflippers to steer and hindflippers to push, or foreflippers to swim and hindflippers to steer.

On land, foreflippers and claws haul the animal forward. In most species, flexible foreflippers are used to scratch or groom.

Internal adaptations have made pinnipeds among the world's best deep-sea divers. Seals can drop their oxygen use by one-third, slowing their heartrate and reducing blood flow. Unlike human beings, they have a high tolerance for carbon dioxide, a toxic by-product of metabolism. Seals also have more hemoglobin in their blood cells and more myoglobin in their muscle cells than we do. Both substances bond with oxygen,

▼ Sea lions have long, leathery hindflippers, used to steer underwater. On land, these flippers turn forward to walk upon.

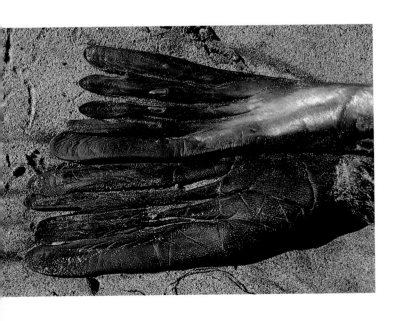

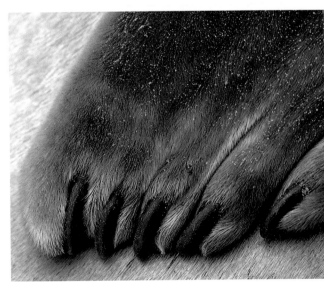

letting them stay underwater longer.

Pinnipeds have special thermostats, too. While sleeping, groups of seals can float, flippers extended into the air like windmill blades. Their flippers contain blood vessels called capillaries. They act as heat dumps to cool the animal, or solar panels to warm it.

If you could see a lineup of pinniped species, two by two, you'd notice an interesting size difference. In more than half the species, males are huge: two to four times bigger than females. This trait is much more common among species where males compete fiercely over

◄Elephant seal foreflippers look like furry fingers, with wide nails or claws.

▲ Most challenges and battles between northern elephant seal males take place on land. Sometimes, however, they do battle in the water. These two adult males are at prime breeding age, nine to 11 years.

females, and try to mate with many.

Other pinniped species fight very little over females.

Instead, an adult seal will have the same mate for some time. In these societies, male and female seals tend to be the same size. When male pinnipeds don't need to compete, they don't need such male accessories as huge size, tusks, manes, or large bulbous noses.

Harbor seals

*T*he harbor seal, one of 18 kinds of true seals, has a mysterious appeal. Perhaps it's those eloquent, unwinking eyes. That thoughtful gaze seems out of place in such a round, helpless-looking body.

A widespread species, harbor seals inhabit the waters around the Atlantic side of North America and Canada, northern Europe, and Japan through the Aleutian Islands and the Bering Sea.

Along the Pacific coast, from Alaska to Baja California, they were never hunted for fur but were shot as pests, because they competed for the same foods as human beings. Well into the 20th century, bounty hunters shot them by the thousands. Today they may number 400,000 animals.

◄ A harbor seal rests in a quiet coastal bay. To get around on land, it hunches its back and scoots forward. Sometimes it moves by rolling.

► What do harbor seals look for in a place to haul out? Good visibility and quick access to deep water. They often rest on rocks like this, taking turns to watch for predators. It may look uncomfortable, but harbor seals find this balancing act easy and normal.

▲ Harbor seals live many places. Some populations are found in cold climates like Alaska or Norway. They often haul out onto sea ice that isn't attached to land.

A harbor seal may be four to six feet long, and weigh anywhere from 70 to 300 pounds. It tends to haul out on terrain similar to its markings. A shy animal that basks without moving, it's easy to mistake its spotted coat of silver-gray or brown for a plump rock.

Typically, this animal has a round head, no neck, and no external ears. On land, it often lies on its belly, foreflippers hugging its body, hindflippers in the air. It looks like a fat little ship left high and dry by the tide. More often, it resembles a whole fleet of such ships; harbor seals frequently rest in groups, while one or two seals take turns keeping watch.

At times, this seal rests in shallow waters, alone or with company. It can even sleep upright in the sea, with just its nostrils showing. This behavior is called bottling.

Harbor seals need to be on dry land, or near it, to molt, give birth, and care for pups. That's why they spend so much time ashore, hauling out onto river banks, sandy or cobblestone beaches, rocky points, and manmade objects like buoys and docks. It's

▼ These two harbor seals are molting. As they rest on rocky shorelines, they let the ocean wash over them. It's hard to tell male from female harbor seals, because they are similar in size.

always astonishing to see how fast they can scoot along on a hard surface, inch-worm fashion.

In liquid, the harbor seal becomes a marine ballerina, spiraling and spinning. As it shimmies along, this swimmer may reach 15 miles per hour. To hunt, the harbor seal sinks slowly to about 300 feet, holding its breath up to 30 minutes as it forages. Harbor seals sometimes travel away from home to fish where prey is seasonally available. During salmon runs, for example, they cluster at the mouths of rivers that flow into the Pacific.

A mature harbor seal is capable of eating five to ten percent of its body weight daily. Swallowing most of its catch whole, it dines on many species of fish, octopus, squid, and smaller creatures.

Quiet compared to other pinnipeds,

▲ Harbor seals have short, webbed foreflippers, tipped with claws. They pull the animal forward on land. In the ocean, its foreflippers help steer.

harbor seals nevertheless have a vocabulary of barks, snorts, and moans. Pups make bleating cries while their mothers are at sea. We've recently learned that harbor seals also communicate underwater. Males in particular roar and grunt, during the mating season and beyond.

Many pinnipeds migrate, but harbor seals do not. Their favorite hauling-out area is home base. They breed and give birth about the same time and place each year. Pupping season falls between March and September, depending on location.

Females give birth on land or water to a single pup, two to three feet long. This gangly baby has weak hindquarters but can nurse, swim, and dive right away. During the four-week nursing period, harbor seals are devoted mothers. When they need to hunt, they stash their pups on the beach.

To a human observer, these pups may seem like orphans—but their solitude is only temporary.

By the time the pup has started solid food, it has doubled its weight, put on a layer of blubber, and become quite self-sufficient. Females now leave the weaned pups and join the males.

By pinniped standards, the social behavior of harbor seals is civilized. Males don't openly fight over females or territory. Instead, they court females by calling and slapping the water with their flippers. After linking with females in courtship pairs, the couples may leap in and out of the sea for some time. During this play, the female will bite the male on the neck and shoulders, often leaving scars.

Harbor seals mate in ocean waters, the female becoming pregnant soon after. She may also breed with additional males. A year later, she will give birth. In her lifetime, a harbor seal can produce 15 offspring.

In the wild, a harbor seal may survive 20 to 35 years, its only enemies being orcas, sharks, and human beings.

▶Harbor seal females usually have their young on land, at their favorite hauling-out place. During the pup's first month, mother and pup spend much time together. At first, the baby's fur is black, blending well with the sea plants on which it rests.

▲ Steller's sea lions, also known as northern sea lions, are heavier and furrier than their California cousins. Males weigh up to 2,400 pounds, with thick manes. They make a deep roar. California sea lions have a higher, sharper bark.

The California sea lion is a noisy extrovert: curious, clever, and excitable. With its collie-dog muzzle, sleek brown body, and sharp bark, it's the animal most people have in mind when they think of a seal. Understandable, since there are more of this species in captivity than any other pinniped.

California sea lions like each others' company. They often bask in tightly massed sunning groups. Juvenile or yearling sea lions, noticeable for their light fur, wiggle in among the darker adults. Females and juveniles have slimmer, more doglike heads and muzzles. In these resting groups, adult males, their bulgy heads often adorned with a sagittal crest, try to intimidate with their magnificence. They pose endlessly with chests out and heads up, emitting loud barks from time to time.

These animals are closely related to four other sea lions, including the Steller's, and nine species of fur seals. All of them have external ears that often look like curled leaves.

But the most noticeable difference between these eared seals and the true seals is the way they move on land. Eared seals make better use of their front and back limbs. On land, a sea lion or fur seal can turn its hind flippers around to sit on them, much as a dog sits on its haunches. To get from place to place, it rears up on its foreflippers and gallops along in a lunging, plunging fashion. Sea lions are so agile they can scramble up cliffs and travel inland for some distance. They even climb stairs!

Underwater, sea lions and fur seals use their strong foreflippers to soar, almost the same way a bird uses its wings. Hindflippers serve as rudders. Sea lions can easily hit 15 miles an hour—then pour it on for short bursts up to 30 miles per hour. Their diving skills are superb, as they can submerge to 1,500 feet or more under water.

Most active of the Pacific coast pinnipeds, California sea lions spend hours at play.

▼ Social sea lions congregate in large groups and often frolic underwater. Females like this one may also flee from danger by letting their young ride piggyback.

They bullet from the sea, flying through the air, dolphin-style—sometimes in unison. A favorite sport is body surfing. Other sea lion activities include bubble chasing, kelp tossing, and sparring in mock battles, using their long rubbery necks. It's no wonder sea lions find it easy to learn ball-balancing, ladder-climbing, and other tricks as performing pinnipeds.

In summer and fall, adult males migrate from the rookeries or breeding grounds in search of prey, accompanied by juveniles of both sexes. These ocean migrations may take them as far north as Canada and as far south as Mexico. As rest stops, sea lions use small offshore rocks and islands along the entire California coast.

In late spring, a California sea lion male returns to the rookery and establishes his territory on the breeding beach, where he corners ten or more females for mating purposes—or tries to. First, though, he must confront other males to win his turf. Males who fail to make it through the semi-final battles are forced out and may never get to breed. What with fights and mating activities, successful males do not eat for two months or more.

In contrast, California sea lion females are stay-at-homes. Once they reach sexual maturity around age five, they remain in

◄ A sleek wet California sea lion hauls out onto a rocky shoreline. Since it's able to raise its body and use all four flippers, it moves faster on land than a harbor seal.

▶ In their first year of life, sea lions have nearly blonde fur. They often rest near other pinniped species, like these elephant seals. Young sea lions have a puppy-like trust in the kindness of strangers.

the breeding and pupping areas year-round. Main rookeries are the offshore islands of Baja California and the Channel Islands.

The dark pups are born in May through July. Once they are ten days old, their mothers go to sea to feed and may be gone several days between nursings. Three weeks after giving birth, females mate with the newly-arrived males. Meanwhile, the sea lion pups keep busy, learning to swim in tidepools, and later soloing in the sea.

California sea lions are among the hungriest of pinnipeds, which often puts them in conflict with commercial fisheries. Females weigh 200 to 300 pounds; males can get over 800 pounds. These adept hunters go after hake, herring, anchovies, flatfish, small sharks, octopus, crab, and lamprey eel. And they rarely miss.

The strangest item in their diet? Stones. Most pinnipeds have the odd habit of rock-eating—but sea lions take the prize. Biologists have found as many as 100 stones, gravel to golf-ball size, in some sea lions' stomachs. Do they help the animal digest its food? Get rid of the parasites that bother many sea lions? No one knows. Perhaps stones ease hunger pangs during the foodless periods that many pinnipeds endure in their breeding and nursing cycles.

▶ Sea lion females nurse their pups for six months—longer than most pinnipeds. Females are lighter in color than males. They are also lighter in weight—one-quarter the size.

Two elephant seals rest together on the beach. With their nimble foreflippers, these animals can groom, toss sand, and even make a "Look at me!" gesture.

▲ An elephant seal female lets a juvenile, perhaps one of her older offspring, stay close. Smooth fur shows that they have recently molted, shedding their old skin and hair.

T he pinniped that has won the biggest fan club of human beings in recent years is the extraordinary elephant seal. There are two species, located at opposite ends of the world.

The southern elephant seal, largest pinniped on the planet, lives in icy waters and on the lonelier islands and beaches of Antarctica, Argentina, and New Zealand. Nearly extinct in the 19th century, the southern population has rebounded to more than half a million animals.

The northern elephant seal population lives in the waters off Alaska, along the Pacific coast, and south to Baja California. Also reduced by human slaughter to near zero, it has slowly repopulated its range. An estimated 150,000 animals now breed on island rookeries like the Farallones, the

Channel Islands, and the Mexican islands of Guadalupe and San Benito. At Ano Nuevo and Piedras Blancas, elephant seals have also established breeding beaches on the mainland.

Why is the elephant seal so fascinating? Partly because it is big, bold, and bizarre-looking. An adult male of the southern species may reach 8,000 pounds and outweigh a truck. Northern animals are smaller but you wouldn't call them trim: 900 to 2,000 pounds for a female, 3,000 to 5,000 pounds for a male. Nearly a ton of that weight is pure blubber. Before electricity replaced oil lamps, seal hunters used to boil down the blubber of elephant seals. One male carcass produced 200 gallons of high-quality lamp oil.

Then there's that nose. As pups, northern elephant seals have huge adorable eyes and short muzzles with a couple of nostrils at the end. As males enter puberty, however, their noses go from cute to colossal. By the time a male matures, its lumpy nose looks like an alien growth, as much as two feet long. Unlike an elephant's trunk, this seal's nose doesn't do much except intimidate other males. Bigger noses awe rivals, avoid fights, and win more opportunities for their owners to mate and father pups.

Although thick-bodied southern elephant seals are nearly double the weight of northern males, their noses are unexpectedly small and ordinary.

All pinnipeds vocalize but elephant seals produce a jarring array of sound effects. The female growls, screams, and calls to keep track of her pup. When arguing with her neighbors, complaining about pups who are milk thieves, or being mated, she also makes a loud, retching gargle. Pups mew, screech, and whine for milk. When separated from their mothers, as is often the case, they make a squealing cry. When tumbled or trampled by adult males with battle on their minds, pups protest, adding to the din.

But the most memorable vocals come from the adult male. From his throat, the male produces a series of booming snorts and explosive burps that carry half a mile or more. His call has a mechanical echo, like someone warming up a chainsaw or an out-of-tune motorcycle. As the male

▲ Big noses show who's boss in an elephant seal rookery. By a male's eighth birthday, his nose has grown to full glory. Noisy threats keep actual battles to a minimum.

▲ To learn more about elephant seal migrations, researchers track animals by marking them with harmless solutions. When molting occurs each year, the name tags must be put on again.

calls, his great nose wobbles and vibrates. Even with a closeup view of the animal, it's still hard to believe those loud sounds are coming out of it. Most vocalizations are threats or challenges to other males, since they compete fiercely over females.

Each rookery or breeding area of elephant seals develops slightly different sound effects. Arrivals from another rookery soon learn to snort, whimper, belch, and scream like the locals.

Despite their bulk, elephant seals move swiftly. When rivals sound a challenge and undulate toward one another, they look like a pair of kingsize traveling waterbeds. Their mobility comes from an extremely flexible backbone, which allows them to lift their great bodies and hunch forward with the help of their foreflippers. Elephant

seals can go vertical too, climbing sand dunes that are steep even by human standards.

Using technology, biologists have tracked elephant seals for long periods. They've learned that each year, these able swimmers do an eye-popping double migration of up to 18,000 miles at sea.

These findings also mean that most of the time, elephant seals live solitary lives, swimming and feeding many miles from land. When not fasting on shore, an elephant seal eats heartily, diving deep to catch rays, small sharks, and rockfish. Three-quarters of its diet, however, is squid. Its intestines are 600 feet long, helping it digest its food in a quick six hours.

November through March, males and females come together to breed and give birth. Most of their rookeries are on remote, uninhabited islands off California. But on the mainland, a growing number of lucky people get to witness this astonishing cycle.

In late November, adult males, also known as bulls, arrive: fit, fat, and ready to do battle. They challenge one another with vocal threats, and display their noses. Most fights end there. When bulls do fight, they slam chest to chest, slashing with their teeth. Battles get bloody but are rarely fatal. Chest shields of callused skin protect the bulls from serious damage. Most battles last a few minutes, often ending with a nose bite or a chase into the sea. But fights between equally matched males may take an hour.

Winners of these battles establish a pecking order, called a dominance hierarchy. Males with the biggest string of victories are called alpha bulls. Most are at prime breeding age—nine to 11 years.

▼ Two full-grown males do battle on the sands at Ano Nuevo State Reserve. Elephant seal males fight to see who becomes number one, known as the alpha bull. When all the females arrive, the alpha bull will be the master of the beach.

▶ Scrawny elephant seal pups soon grow plump on milk four times daily. Over 50 percent of it is fat—the richest milk from any mammal mother. For each pound the pup gains, the mother loses two.

◄ When her baby is born, an elephant seal mother warbles to it. The pup calls back. The two sniff each other. This is called imprinting. This behavior bonds mother and pup.

By December, when the pregnant females arrive, one by one, the males have sorted themselves out. At the top is a small group of alpha bulls—sometimes just one or two. Next in rank are the beta bulls. Lowest ranking are young males called bachelor bulls. Females quickly join harems, each group of 25 to 50 protected by an alpha bull to keep other males away.

Four to six days later, each female gives birth to a 60 to 80-pound pup. The two bond by sniffing and warbling. Without this imprinting of newborn and mother, the pup would starve because its mother would fail to recognize it.

▼ Orphan pups, like this one crying near a male elephant seal, usually die. Sometimes, a female will adopt an orphan—or it will learn to steal milk from her.

◄ To mate, an elephant seal gets behind a female, slings his foreflipper over her, and bites her neck. She responds by vocalizing.

Born with a wrinkled black coat, the wobbly pup nurses greedily, soon filling out. In four weeks, pups quadruple their birth weight while their mothers shrink. For each pound gained by the pup, the female loses two.

Crowds and noise make the rookery dangerous. Pups aren't very mobile, and mothers can do little to protect them. Some are accidentally squashed. Others are killed by unfriendly adults.

After a pup nurses for three weeks, its mother comes into estrus for four days, and is ready to breed. The alpha bull of her harem promptly mates with her, and she becomes pregnant again. Since every alpha bull's goal is to mate with as many females as possible, he eats nothing during this 90-day period in order to mate as many as 200 times.

To breed, elephant seals lie on the sand. The male gets behind the female, slings a foreflipper across her, bites her neck, and mates. If she protests, he may bite harder and puts his weight on her—possibly crushing a pup that's too close.

No matter how alert the alpha bull is, he can't always guard the females at the edge of his harem. Sometimes he lets a few beta males hang around to keep the bachelor bulls away. If lucky, a beta bull may win a chance to mate while the alpha is busy, or resting.

When the female is not ready, or when approached by a male that isn't alpha material, she lets out a shriek. Other females in the harem often take up her protest cry.

To survive this intense period, adult elephant seals rest frequently. In rest mode, they use their foreflippers to toss sand over their backs—the only pinnipeds to cool themselves this way. To save energy, they are also able to stop breathing for up to 30 minutes.

When pups reach one month or so, they are weaned. Their mothers simply head for the water. It takes the females awhile to escape, since excited males, especially the lower ranking betas and bachelor bulls, try to stop them. Some alpha bulls escort the female to the sea, but most do little to protect her. Even in the water, the thin, exhausted mother often has to fight off unwelcome attention.

By March, much worse for wear, male and female adults head for the sea. There they go their own ways, foraging for squid and other protein to regain strength.

Meanwhile, the newly-weaned pups remain at the rookery. Clustered in groups called pods, the weaners venture into shallow waters, learning to swim and catch prey. As they grow bigger and leaner, their fur changes to silvery-gray. By June, the

▲ After elephant seal mothers cut off the milk supply to their pups, they leave for the sea. The weaned pups stay on shore, in groups called pods. Together, they learn to swim and catch prey.

weaners leave for their first solo trip in the open sea. Only half will survive; the rest will end up in the stomachs of sharks and orcas.

In late spring, females return to shore to molt. Among elephant seals, this is a startling process. Other creatures shed skin or hair, but this is a catastrophic molt. Big sheets of skin, with hair attached, fall off; the animals appear sick. During this month, females rest close together, staying warm while new hair grows in.

Adult males return to land in summer for their molt. On the beach, they hang out in groups, later moving into the water to swim, vocalize, and carry out friendly mock battles. During the fall, some juveniles and younger adults will come ashore to molt. But mature elephant seals will not return to breed again until November.

▶ In shallow water, young elephant seals fight mock battles, preparing for the competition they will find as adult males. They gargle, roar, and grunt, imitating the adults.

▼ Each year, elephant seals shed big chunks of skin and hair all at once. This natural process, called a catastrophic molt, looks strange but does not hurt the animal.

Seals around the world

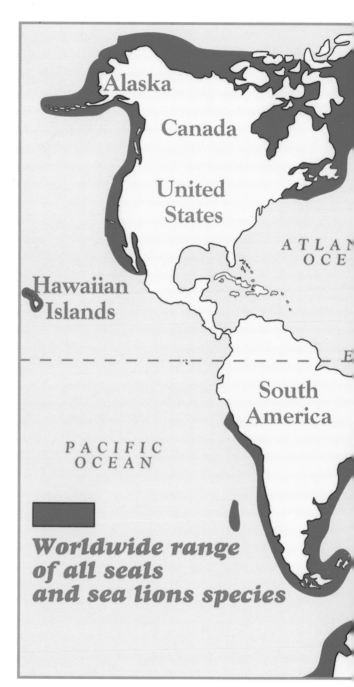

Worldwide range of all seals and sea lions species

▲ The sleek crabeater seal is the most plentiful pinniped in the world, and the fastest on land. It lives on pack ice around Antarctica. Instead of crab, it eats large amounts of tiny shellfish called krill.

T he 33 species of pinnipeds have settled in diverse habitats, making adaptations that are just as diverse.

The Baikal seal, for instance, is named after its home: the world's deepest lake, in Russia. During the Siberian winter, Lake Baikal gets covered with three feet of ice. To fish, Baikal seals make breathing holes in it. Females use snowdrifts to give birth—at times, to twins.

The Baikal seal is the only seal species that lives in fresh water all the time. However, some harbor seals hunt for seasonal prey by swimming into rivers or fresh-water lakes, such as the well-named Seal Lake in Canada.

The most abundant seal in the world is the crabeater, a species found on the shifting pack ice around Antarctica. Instead of eating crab as you might expect, it lives on krill, a small crustacean that schools in huge numbers underwater. There may be

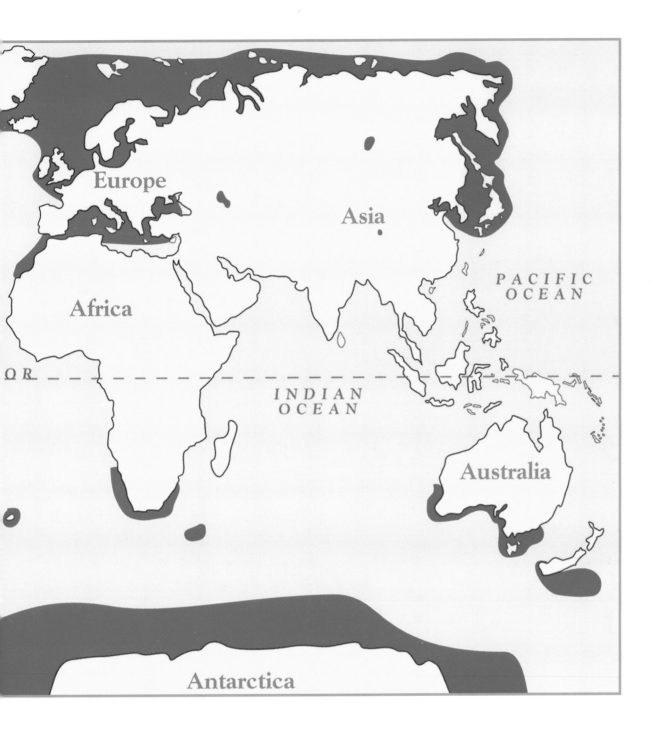

as many as 40 million crabeater seals, more than all the other species put together. The crabeater also happens to be the fastest pinniped on land.

Another misnamed species is the bearded seal. Instead of a beard, this seal wears a fancy mustache. It lives on the drifting sea ice around the Arctic Circle, diving to pick mollusks, worms, and shrimp off the bottom. Exciting research is being done on the complex songs sung underwater by this animal.

Not all seals favor cold climates. The harbor seal ranges as far south as Mexico and Florida, and into Portugal on the Atlantic side. The Mediterranean monk seal, now greatly endangered, hauls out in North Africa and other southern points. The gray seal is found in the British Isles. Sea lions also live off the coasts of Peru, Chile, and Brazil. Even the Hawaiian Islands has its own species of monk seal, although its numbers near extinction.

▲ Elephant seals are wild animals. Even if they look sick or tame, they should never be approached except by wildlife professionals. Here, a researcher measures a female.

*I*n the wild, pinnipeds get eaten by polar bears on ice, or by orcas and sharks in the water. Pups also fall prey to wolves, bald eagles, coyotes —and other seals.

But modern life holds bigger dangers. Although demand for seal fur has fallen steeply, a few nations continue to cull or weed out certain species. In 2004, over 320,000 baby harp seals and hooded seals were legally killed for their delicate fur on the ice floes of Canada and Greenland.

Most of us no longer kill pinnipeds deliberately; but as ocean explorer and environmentalist Jacques Cousteau once said, we have yet to stop killing the ocean itself, the mother of all life.

Hundreds of thousands of pinnipeds die from entanglement in fishing nets and plastic bands. Most drown, or slowly die of wounds that choke off blood circulation. Human populations clash and compete with seals over salmon and catch from the sea or rivers. Habitat fragmentation and loss of breeding grounds threaten pinniped well-being. Global warming literally melts away seal pupping areas on land ice and pack

ice. Some widespread pollutants, such as the organochlorines DDT and PCB, cause huge failures to reproduce in female seals.

Groups like Friends of the Elephant Seal and the Seal Conservation Society promote education and understanding of these marine miracles. Global organizations like Earthwatch connect volunteers with scientists in the field, working on sustainable ways to preserve pinniped habitat and species. Entities like the Monterey Bay National Marine Sanctuary protect and manage rich aquatic and land resources for public use, including the mainland breeding sites for elephant seals in California. Other human allies and agencies clean up the seas, making them safer for seals—such as the four-year project that collected 40 tons of torn fishing nets from the reefs of Hawaii.

Since we stopped killing off most pinnipeds for fur, blubber, and dogfood, we've discovered the value of cooperating with these trusting creatures. Most of us know seals and sea lions as trained

▲ Young seals are curious. When they play with fishing nets, plastic, and other hazards thrown into the ocean by people, they sometimes get caught in them. As this elephant seal grows bigger, the plastic it wears may kill it.

performers or lovable residents of marine aquariums. But they are valuable friends to us as well. They've been taught to help divers in trouble, retrieve equipment, and perform other deepwater tasks beyond human capabilities. Medical researchers are intensely studying their abilities and adaptations, work that may one day be used to make our lives healthier.

The rest of the world's creatures, pinnipeds included, are as deserving of life as we are. By making sure these fascinating animals survive, we maintain nature's balance—and do ourselves a big favor.

- In a land race, the crabeater seal could easily beat a human runner.

- While at sea, a pregnant pinniped can postpone the birth date of her pup until she returns to land—a neat trick called delayed implantation.

- Elephant seals can dive one mile deep— more than ten times deeper than a human diver can go.

- Walruses love clams, and suck them right out of their shells. It takes a thousand clams to make a single walrus meal.

- All pinnipeds wear blubber under their skins. The layer of fat on a sea lion may be three inches thick.

- The champs at holding their breath underwater are elephant seals—their record is two hours.

- All pinnipeds swallow rocks. Some sea lions have 50 pounds of stones in their stomachs. No one knows why, either.

- Each year, elephant seals swim up to 18,000 miles in a double migration.

▼ At water's edge on the California coast, elephant seal bulls challenge each other with loud threats. Usually, one male backs down. If not, the two fight, chest to chest, for dominance.

▲ The "top dog" among northern elephant seals is called an alpha male. When on land, he stays alert. He protects 25 to 50 female seals while they give birth. The alpha male tries to mate with all of them.

Glossary

Alpha bull. The dominant male or males among pinnipeds. At the breeding grounds, an alpha bull guards a group or harem of females while they give birth, then mates with as many as possible.

Bachelor bull. The lowest ranking male in a pinniped breeding group, usually a younger animal. With age and size, bachelors may become beta bulls. Only a rare few ever become alphas.

Beta bull. A male pinniped, secondary to the alpha bull. In his life, a beta may become a better fighter and win alpha status.

Bottling. The sleeping behavior of harbor seals and other pinnipeds. They rest upright in the sea, with only their nostrils visible.

Blubber. A thick layer of fat beneath the skin of many marine mammals. In pinnipeds, blubber insulates, protects, and nourishes the animal.

Chest shield. Among elephant seals, an area of thickened skin on the chest that protects adult males from injury during battles.

Delayed implantation. The ability of a pregnant seal to stop the development of an embryo within her body. This allows her to give birth in pupping season, usually onshore.

Dominance hierarchy. In many pinniped and other animal societies, a way of organization by which a few enjoy more power than the many. Among elephant seals, only a few of the highest ranking males get to mate with most or all of the females.

Estrus. The period of time when female pinnipeds are receptive to mating, usually when onshore at the rookery or breeding beach.

Harem. A group of females guarded by a dominant or alpha male while they give birth. They are later mated by the same bull.

Hauling out. Coming out of water onto rocks, ice, or land.

Imprinting. Actions, such as vocalizing and sniffing, that bond a seal mother and pup so she will later recognize it. This occurs right after the pup is born.

Krill. Shrimplike creatures, up to two inches long, abundant in cold seas around Antarctica and the main food for some whales and pinnipeds.

Molting. The annual shedding of fur or skin, occurring in many animals. Pinnipeds like the elephant seal have a catastrophic molt, where sheets of skin and clumps of hair come off all at once.

Opportunistic carnivore. A flesh-eating animal that hunts whatever prey is available.

Orca. A member of the whale family (cetacean) commonly known as a killer whale, which hunts some seal species.

Parasites. Tiny organisms living in or on the bodies of animals, such as sea lions. They may cause sickness or death.

Pod. A group of young pinnipeds, such as elephant seals, after being weaned from their mothers' milk.

Rookery. A breeding ground or beach where male and female pinnipeds meet each year to mate and give birth.

Undulate. To move in a wiggly, wavy fashion, like a caterpillar or a true seal on land, such as the elephant seal.

Weaners. An elephant seal from the time it is weaned to its first migration at sea, about three months.

Yearling. A young pinniped that has experienced its first migration and its first return onshore.

About the author

Vicki León, Series Editor of the London Town Wild Life Series, has written 31 books, including titles on sea otters, killer whales, wetlands, octopuses, and parrots in the wild.

Photographers

Much-published wildlife photographer, naturalist, and park ranger Frank Balthis did 34 stirring photos for this book, including the cover shot. Other photographers contributed ten more images: Ralph A. Clevenger, pp 14, 15; Howard Hall, pp 7, 8, 21; Richard R. Hansen, pp 9, 12-13; W. E. Townsend, Jr., back cover, pp 22-23, 25 bottom..

Special thanks

- Michele Roest, Outreach & Education Specialist, Monterey Bay National Marine Sanctuary
- Joni Hunt, special research
- Michael Putman
- Sheri Howe
- Ano Nuevo Interpretive Association
- California State Park Rangers
- Faculty and researchers at UC Santa Cruz Institute of Marine Science

Where to view seals, sea lions & elephant seals

Remember, pinnipeds are protected species and wild animals. It's exciting to photograph them, but don't get too close. Disturbing them is against the law, and unsafe as well.

- **In the wild:** In Alaska: the Inland Passage; the Aleutian Islands. In British Columbia: the Inland Passage; around Vancouver Island. In Washington: Puget Sound and the San Juan Islands; the mouth of the Columbia River. In Oregon: at the mouths of the Columbia and Rogue Rivers; Sea Lion Caves. In California: recommended places with interpretive guides: rookeries at Point Reyes National Seashore at elephant seal lookout near Chimney Rock; Point Lobos State Park; Ano Nuevo State Park and Reserve; and Piedras Blancas, north of San Simeon. Other seal watching spots: the mouth of the Russian River, near Jenner; Monterey wharf; Santa Cruz wharf; Elkhorn Slough in Moss Landing; Pier 39 and Seal Rock in San Francisco; along the Big Sur coast; Cayucos Pier; Avila Pier; Montana de Oro State Park, near Morro Bay; the Channel Islands.
- **In captivity:** Most zoos and aquaria have seals and sea lions on display. Go to the following website for details on special exhibits in your area, or the places you plan to visit: www.aza.org. Select AZA Zoos & Aquariums, then select by state or alphabetical order. This is a partial list only.
- Vancouver Aquarium, British Columbia, Canada; Seattle Aquarium, WA; Oregon Coast Aquarium, Newport OR; San Francisco Zoo and Aquarium of the Bay, San Francisco CA; Monterey Bay Aquarium, Monterey CA; Aquarium of the Pacific, Long Beach CA; Sea World, San Diego CA; Waikiki Aquarium, Honolulu HI.
- Shedd Aquarium, Chicago IL; Audubon Zoo, New Orleans LA; Aquarium for Wildlife Conservation, Brooklyn NY; Virginia Marine Science Museum, Virginia Beach VA.
- Outside North America: Chester Zoo, England; Osaka Aquarium, Japan; Sydney Aquarium, Australia.

Helping organizations and good websites

- Friends of the Elephant Seal: office at 250 San Simeon Ave. Suite 3B, San Simeon, CA 93452. (805) 924-1628. Mail: PO Box 490, Cambria CA 93428. Community-based volunteer organization educates, sponsors programs, and has docents on hand year-round at the elephant seal rookery south of Piedras Blancas. Useful, kid-friendly website, with lots of good links: (www.elephantseal.org)
- Ano Nuevo State Reserve, Highway One, San Mateo County, 55 miles south of San Francisco; (650) 879-0227, (800) 444-4445. Interpretive program conducts guided walks for public and school tours, at the first mainland breeding colony for northern elephant seals. (www.parks.ca.gov/parkindex)
- Monterey Bay National Marine Sanctuary. One of 13 in the U.S., this marine sanctuary protects 276 miles of critical California coastline and nearshore, including both mainland elephant seal rookeries. MBNMS operates interpretive centers, sponsors Ocean Fairs, puts on community education programs. Along coastal Highway One, there are vista points and rich opportunities to see pinnipeds from elephant seals to sea lions. (www.mbnms.nos.noaa.gov)
- The Marine Mammal Center, Operates rescue and rehab for pinnipeds; has a volunteer program. The website includes teacher resources and links to aquaria and helping agencies. (www.marinemammalcenter.org)
- Seal Conservation Society. British-based membership group provides information and statistics about species worldwide. Good website with database and list of pinniped welfare and conservation organizations. (www.pinnipeds.org)
- Earthwatch Institute, 3 Clock Tower Place, #100, Maynard MA 01754. Superb website: www.earthwatch.org. Kids can become members, learn about ongoing field work to save pinniped species, oceans, and habitats in jeopardy. Ages 16 and up can take part in over 150 expeditions each year.
- Monterey Bay Aquarium, 886 Cannery Row, Monterey CA 93950. Incredibly rich website, with untold resources for kids, teachers, parents. (www.mbayaq.org)

To learn more

Books

- *National Audubon Society Guide to Marine Mammals of the World,* by Randall R. Reeves, et al. (Knopf Publishing Group, 2002) Best all-around reference, with species by species chapters, range maps, photos, illustrations & glossary. Covers whales, otters, polar bears, and manatees also.
- *Seals and Sea Lions of the World,* by Nigel Bonner. (Facts on File, 2004) Great reference, dense text, organ-

ized by pinniped families, with useful subheads and much on human-seal relations. Good photos; some may be too graphic for younger readers.

- *Seals,* by Ron Hirschi. (Benchmark Books, 2003). Very good book for younger readers; high-quality photos.
- *Fur Seals and Other Pinnipeds,* by Lome Piasetsky. (World Book, 2000). Easy text for kids, good info, excellent photos.

Videos & DVDs

- "Elephant Seals of Piedras Blancas." Side-off Video, 2000. VHS and DVD. 70 minutes. Amazing footage of a year in the life of the elephant seal colony and breeding grounds near Piedras Blancas lighthouse in San Luis Obispo County, CA. On-camera interviews with leading biologists add richness.
- "Elephant Seals of Año Nuevo." California State Parks/San Mateo County Natural History Association, 1994. VHS. 30 minutes. Useful film, interesting footage of the breeding colony at Ano Nuevo.
- "World's Last Great Places: Antarctica, the Last Wilderness." National Geographic, 1993. VHS. 60 minutes. Classic look at how elephant seals, crabeater seals, and other species survive and thrive in this hostile climate.
- "Kamchatka." PBS Living Edens series, 1999. VHS. 60 minutes. Excellent footage on the fur seal; the film also spends much time on bears, salmon, and seabirds.

▼ Near Piedras Blancas lighthouse on California's central coast, thousands of northern elephant seals come ashore each year to molt, mate, and give birth. This rookery attracts many thousands of human visitors. They get to see an astonishing wildlife show.

Index

Photographs are numbered in **boldface** and follow the print references after **PP** (photo page).